A Symphony In My Soul

A Rhapsody Of Poetic Words

Selected Poems

Elouise Matthews

Foreword by
Margaret Morenike Doherty

Dedication

*I*t is with great joy that I dedicated this book to my family: My husband, Stephen Anthony, and three children, Stephanie Antoinette, Cheryl Louise, and Isaac Alexander. With my deepest appreciation, I dedicate this book to my mother, Ida Mae, and father, Tommy Brandy Jr., my mother-in law, Cipriana, and father-in law, Augustus Henry Matthews, and to my grandparents and my husband's grandparents.

Table of Contents

Instructional

Biographical and Historical

Romantic

Inspirational

Foreword

*M*rs. Elouise Matthews is a friend and a student of the word of God. For the short time that I've known her, it is evident that her faith is built up in the word of God. She is a follower of the Lord Jesus Christ. Elouise is an Educator who has taught Reading for the past thirty years but more importantly, she is a teacher of the word of God. The Holy Spirit is teaching and showing her how to use the training that she has received as a Reading Specialist and Writing Consultant to understand, enlighten, and write spiritual, prophetic, and inspirational poems.

The finger of God has touched her soul. The poems that Elouise writes uplifts the soul of every man, woman, boy or girl who reads them. These poems will water and feed every soul and spirit with the infallible word of God. God's word said that it would restore our souls and cause them to prosper, Psalm 23:3 and 3 John 2.

The saving of the soul by shining the light of God's word within it, and restoring love, joy, and peace ring throughout her poems. While some poets write out of their painful experiences and suffering, in A Symphony In My Soul, Mrs. Elouise Matthews writes a collection of poems about hope, promise, love, encouragement, praise, prayer, kingdom seekers, the family, and many, many more. The prophet Jeremiah stated in Jeremiah 15:16, that "God's words were found, and he ate them; and God's word was unto him the joy and rejoicing of his heart (soul)." This in essence is the message that is echoing in her poems. Elouise rejoices as her soul looks back into the chapters of her life to see what God has done for her and presses onward as God writes new chapters in her life. Her soul has its hope in God and she praises Him more and more, Psalm 42:5, and Psalm 71:14. Her words are like the fragrant from a flower coming from a grateful and a rejoicing heart. Elouise delivers a message of hope as in "Your Future Is Bright" to a holy cheer in "Honey There Ain't Nothing Like Church."

As you read these poems, let the beauty, sweetness, and purity fill your heart and soul with light and life. These poems speak of the goodness, grace, and the love of God. The gift of poetry – the gift of words - is a good gift that comes from the Almighty God. Elouise uses her God given gift to uplift the souls of mankind. Poetic beauty flows from her soul. She has programmed her mind by reading the word of God and thus her mind thinks in line with the word of God which is manifested throughout her poems.

I encourage you the reader to read the entire collection of poems and be blessed. Receive inspiration, instruction, understanding, and encouragement into your heart and soul as you read A Symphony In My Soul. Futhermore, I encourage you to tell others about this collection of poems that will be a blessing to them as well.

Margaret Morenike Doherty

Acknowledgements

I would like to first thank God for the gift of His Word, the gift of his son, and for the gift of creativity and poetic words. Thank you Jesus the Christ for being my Saviour, Lord, and Life, and the Holy Spirit for being my teacher, comforter, and my Helper. I thank my husband, Stephen, who encouraged me to publish this collection of poems. I will always cherish the collection of poetry books that you have given to me over the years. I thank grandmother Mary who passed on the love of poetry to me. I thank my mentors: Phyllis Wheatley, Maya Angelou, Nikki Giovanni, and Eloise Greenfield for blazing the trail for others to follow. A special and most grateful thanks to my editor, Mrs. Margaret Morenike Doherty, for her excellent writing and editing skills. We have communicated through e-mails over the past several months. She is a spiritual writer, a teacher of the Word of God, as well as a full time Nurse. I am blessed to have Margaret as my dear friend and godly sister.

I would like to thank my spiritual mentors, Apostle Nike Daramy for her prayers and spiritual boldness, and for publishing my poems in the Messenger and the church bulletin, and Pastor Jacqueline McCullough for her spiritual frankness and sense of humor, whom I try to hear and see whenever she comes to town, and Pastor Joyce Meyers, I'm blessed by all of the books that she has written. Thank you Mrs. Vivienne Anderson for your meek and gentle spirit and for taking the time to read the collection of poems and for providing your comments and encouraging words. It's good to personally know someone else who writes spiritual and inspirational poems. Thank you Holy Spirit for leading me to my poetic sister! Thank you Bishop Anderson for encouraging me to write a poem about "Where are the Giant Slayers?" I will dedicate it to you when it is completed.

I thank my sister, friends, and prayer partners for their support: Edith Young, Curtis Osborne, Beverly William Cleaves, Helen Hannah, Cheryl McAfee Mitchell, Rosalind Baylor, Juanita Douglas, Linda Smith, Ife Johnson, Yvonne Evans, Isis Tuel, Rosalind Lynch, Leonor Greenidge, Penelope White, Aree Scott, Betty Ross, Joyce Parker, Terri Allen, Barbara Davis, Hattie Stancil, Elaine Williams, Jeannette Smithson, Lauren Pruden, Marie Wrenn, Lynne Foreman, Duana Petrus, Tracey Collins, and Shermaine Waldon, Kathy Philyaw, Sharon Phox, Jemma Davis, Ronnie Carthan, Mary Scott, Ozaree Twillie, Althea Gibson, and Ericka Reid.

A special thanks to all of the churches and pastors who have contributed to my spiritual growth and development: Sequell Baptist (Pastor Gaines), the church that I grew up in, and my home church, Ebenezer (Pastor Grainger Browning and Pastor Jo

Ann Browning), the stone of help for my family, and the place where my family fellowship and have grown together spiritually, Temple of Praise (Apostle Nike Daramy), the National Church of God (Pastor Lowery), and Action Worship Center (Archbishop Duncan-Williams and Bishop Kathy Ann Samaroo). Finally, I thank God for my spiritual teachers of the Word of God: The late Rev. Kenneth Hagin, Dr. Charles Stanley, Dr. Adrian Rodgers, Apostle Michael Youssef, and Dr. T.D. Jakes. I thank God for your unwavering faith in the infallible Word of God!

Introduction

Symphony *In My Soul* is a collection of poems that I've written over a period of years (from childhood to adulthood). It is my prayer that this collection of poems will minister to your soul and spirit. Allow them to speak to you and shed light into the dark chambers of your soul. They were written to uplift, inspire, provoke, instruct, and to give you hope. This gift of poetic words was given to me by God to use for His kingdom. My imagination and creativity are under the guidance of the Holy Spirit and my soul has been submitted to God, the Father. There is greatness in the imagination. (Eph. 3:20) It is a spiritual and divine gift from the Most High God.

A Symphony In My Soul collection of poems tell of the salvation that has come into my soul. My testimony is spoken of in Psalm 66:16 and it states, "come and hear, all ye that fear God, and I will declare what God hath done for my soul." The theme poem, "There's A Symphony In My Soul and I've just gotta get it out," shouts this message. The word of God says in 1 Peter 5:10, "After you have suffered a little while, our God, who is full of kindness through

Christ, will give you His glory. He personally will come and pick you up, and set you firmly in place, and make you stronger than ever." God redeems our souls, (Psalm 71:23) and He has prepared a place for those of us who will serve and obey Him faithfully on this earth, 1Cor. 2:9, Prov. 19:16.

May God bless A Rhapsody of Poetic Words, from "Confessions For The Soul" to "Wash My Feet, Lord," (Psalm 139:23, 24). May they bless each and every reader and listener. Heavenly Father, I pray in the matchless name of your Son Jesus Christ that you would use this gift of poetic words to draw your people closer to you who alone redeems and saves souls.

I pray that they would allow your Holy word to be their godly guidance and allow their souls to walk in the light of it. As for me, my soul is rich and my life is beautiful all because of You!

There's A Symphony In My Soul

There's a symphony in my soul
 I've just gotta get it out!
There's a symphony in my soul
 I've just gotta get it out!

There's love in my heart
 I've just gotta get it out!
There's love in my heart
 I've just gotta get it out!

There's a blessing in my mouth
 I've just gotta get it out!
There's a blessing in my mouth
 I've just gotta get it out!

There're joy bells ringing in my soul
 I've just gotta shout it out!
There're joy bells ringing in my soul
 I've just gotta shout it out!

Oh what peace that floods my soul
I've just gotta tell about it!
Oh what peace that floods my soul
I've just gotta tell about it!

There's a symphony in my soul
 I've just gotta get it out!
There's a symphony in my soul
 I've just gotta get it out!

A Poetic Flight

Let me take you on a poetic flight,
Just call to confirm your reservation;
Put on your coat and shoes,
For you must not wait until the last moment;
And close the window to keep out the invisible friend.

We're going to see and experience an ocean of fun
in the Motherland,
And take a peek at earth as we fly above the clouds;
You will think you are dreaming but you're not,
All aboard are kingdom seekers
Heading for a family reunion in their homeland.
So stay tuned and await the Master's voice
Because He will speak, just get ready to listen.
Final call, buckle up, and sit tight,
As we soar on this poetic flight.

Music

Music can awaken the imagination and the spirit of
creativity.
It is a treasure, a well, that's buried within.
Music brings healing and comfort to the human spirit,
And influences one's thinking and moves the mouth
to sing.

Music gives wings to the human mind,
And allows the soul to soar where eagles fly,
Reliving precious moments and creating make-believe
worlds,
Renewing, refreshing, and transforming minds.

Music stirs the emotions and ignites the physical
energy,
Incased in the human soul,
Spilling out into the earthly atmosphere,
Creating new beginnings, encouraging, and uplifting
the human spirit,
Bringing peace, joy, and relief to the weary soul.

Music can inspire the spirit to leap into praise and
 rejoicing,
Breaking free of the chain that tries to confine it,
Removing the dark cloud that hovers above it,
And allowing the spirit to soar in heavenly places.
Music is such a blessed thing.

The heart cries if it flows from a melancholy and
downcast spirit,
And laughs as the body dances, if it flows from a
spirit that's been set free.
Music is a gift from God that's meant to be enjoyed
and shared,
It makes life worth living and living a life worthwhile.

Words, Words, Words

Encouragement flows through me to you,
Blessings are released through me to you;
Words of praise creates an atmosphere
That allows me to offer Jesus to you.

A prayer from me to you is sent up to
The one who is the Creator of words;
Words of wisdom, love, prophesy, and inspiration,
Are spoken to inspire, uplift, and provoke emotions,
Feelings, and memories, both positive and pleasant.

So open your ears and hearts to receive,
My offering and gift of poetic words.
For they are spoken in a spirit of truth, love, and joy.
I release them now out of my heart to yours,
And through my lips to your ears.

A Step – A New Beginning

Climb up the seven steps,
One step
At a time,
Because if you fall
You'll have to start
All over again.

Vision

It is not unusual to view things with our natural eyes. In fact, many of us lean heavily on our ability to see things with the physical eyes. For example, a groom looks upon his beautiful future wife as she walks down the aisle; a mother watches her children from the kitchen window, playing in the backyard as she prepares dinner; and a child sees a poodle as his or her special pet at the pet shop.

But, what about the spiritual eyes? Do they develop as one develops physically? Over the years, I have read about, and heard about people, who seem to see beyond their physical eyes. Did Moses' mother possess spiritual eyes, which caused her to disobey the King's decree choosing to save her son who later became the leader of the people? What about Nelson Mandela? As a young lad like Joseph, who in a dream saw his brothers bowing down before him, did he see himself as a ruler over his brothers and sisters in South Africa? How come Albert Einstein's mother could see personal and inner character qualities in him that his teacher couldn't see?

Do artists and architects see things with their spiritual eyes thus creating great masterpieces and amazing works of art that can be seen with the physical eyes? Could in fact Helen Keller's teacher, Ann

Sullivan, have taught Helen, who learned to speak, read, and write in Braille, to use her spiritual eyes since she could neither physically see nor hear? Perhaps Wilma Rudolph's mother saw her daughter, a victim of polio and unable to walk, as a champion runner, which led her to travel hundreds of miles to obtain a physical therapist for Wilma. Could George Washington Carver have seen the many by-products from the peanut and sweet potato during those six days of seclusion in his science laboratory?

Spiritual eyes...my mind continues to ponder this question. Yes, spiritual eyes. Do you have them? Do I have them? Just as one's eyes develop and mature physically, so is it with spiritual eyes.

Each time I review and read Dr. King's speeches, I realize that he too viewed people, things, and the world around him through his spiritual eyes. I'm sure if asked, Ray Charles would agree that one is blessed to be able to see physically, but Helen Keller might strongly agree that to possess spiritual eyes are an even greater wealth than physical ones.

A Legacy Within

An environment - good or bad alone doesn't shape
a destiny,
Or make you who you are, nor does what people
say or think you are.
For the Creator puts within us all the ability to think
and to choose.

Negative circumstances can strengthen and fortify,
And help one to see life's blessings rather than curses.
A lily can grow strong in a field, thriving with
tumble weeds,
For within it lies a will and a determination to live.

At the point of the darkest hour, is the dawning
of a new day,
And a caterpillar is transformed from a crawler to
a soaring butterfly.
Suffering gracefully accepted, prepares one for
life's greatest calling.
The loss of one's eyesight awakens the potential
And puts to flight the healthy senses.

If an oak tree is cut down, it will germinate
and grow again.
The same boiling water that softens a carrot
hardens an egg.
Intense heat purifies gold and silver,
And black is a combination of all colors combined.

The pruning of a rosebush stimulates it
And causes it to produce larger roses.
A beautiful rainbow appears after a rain storm,
And a homeless shelter can be grooming ground for
a great leader.

Man possesses a legacy within,
And there's something in the spirit of man,
That propels him onward and upward,
And that legacy within is a faith and a belief in the
Divine Creator,
And a destiny to fulfill a divine purpose in life.

Your Future Is Bright

Your future is bright saith the Lord,
Because I hold it in My hand;
Come to me and I will tell you of My divine plan.

Your future is bright saith the Lord,
And even though there are enemies in the
promised land,
Rest assured that I am with you;
For I am greater than any demon or man,
And I will fight for you.

Your future is bright saith the Lord,
Because I am the Creator of all things,
And a Miracle Worker too.
 So set sail on My wings,
 Trust, believe, and have faith in Me.

Your future is bright saith the Lord,
And when trouble, famine, sickness, or death,
Knocks on your door, the door is locked tight.
The Holy Spirit, your guard, has the key
And He's standing with an angel on your right.

Your future is bright saith the Lord,
So keep walking by faith and not by sight.
Stay on the path of My divine plan,
As you journey into the promised land,
Because your future is bright saith the Lord.

Dreams

God gives us dreams to visualize
What we can accomplish,
And faith to believe the impossible.

God gives us lives to live out the dreams,
And energy and strength to make them happen.
He hides the dreams within our hearts,
So no one else can claim them as their own.

God gives us words to make known
These dreams to others;
He gives us each day of our lives,
To give life to what lies within our vision.

God left on earth assigned work
For each of us to do.
Then He gave us dreams
To see what's left undone,
And a free will to complete the work,
Or leave it yet undone.

I Am That I Am

I am a wife, a mother, a godmother, a daughter,
a granddaughter,
A god-daughter, a sister, a sister-in-law, an aunt,
a cousin, and a friend.
I am a sacrificer, a giver, a provider, a nurturer,
and a lover.
I am a teacher, a mentor, a student, a writer, a poet,
a dancer, a gardener, and
A fisherman.
I am Elouise Matthews and my name is written
in the Lamb's book of life.
I am that I am.

I am a human being, a woman, a female, an adult,
a spirit, and a miracle
Created by God.
I am saved, delivered, and set free. I am a sheep
in the Master Shepherd's
Pasture.
I am a new creature in Christ and joint heir with
Jesus Christ.
I am the righteous one in Jesus Christ.
I am that I am.

I am a temple of the Almighty God and I am protected
by the Holy Angels.
I am seated together with Christ in heavenly places.
I am a vessel filled with the Holy Spirit. I am an anointed
one. I am salt and light in the world.
I am a forgiver, a prayer warrior who is not of

this world.
I am that I am.

I am blessed in the city and blessed in the field.
I am going to make heaven my eternal home.
I am born of a woman and born of the spirit.
I have the character of Mary, Ruth, and Hannah.
I am royalty. I am the apple of my Father's eyes.
I am a child of the Most High God.
I am that I am.

The Windy Guards

The wind, a mighty force in nature,
That guards the four corners of the earth. An
invisible power, untouchable, of a known source,
With an origin and a birth.

It suddenly appears as a cool breeze,
Dancing gently as it passes you by,
Softly touching your cheeks with a blow,
And lighting down upon your head as a
Refreshing breath of air.

It can announce its presence like a roaring lion,
Destroying everything in its sight and path.
This mighty rushing wind parted the red sea.
When the mission is finished, it becomes a lamb,
As it soars around the earth, tamed at last.

When the season comes, it shows itself
As a whirlwind turning, shifting, and stirring
Things in mid-air, bringing a change in the
physical realm,
Awakening us from sleep and our comfort zones.

It can come on the wings of a voice, a whistle
or a whisper,
Breathing upon the first man and woman,
Moving upon the earth as in the beginning,
Letting us know that it is near,

Bringing new life and peace into our hearts
and minds.

And so the Great Creator summons His guard
That's faithful to the call with honor,
As He looks down to earth and chooses him
On guard, in one of the four corners of the earth.

Jealousy

A razor that cuts
Creating a wound
Leaving a heartache.

A beggar that takes
A thief that steals
A wolf in sheep's clothing.

Covetous, suspicious, envious
A tidal wave that boomerangs
Crucifying, isolating and separating.

An explosive bomb
A deflated balloon
Unleashing toxic air.

A joy breaker, a peace taker
A mistaken identity
A silent killer.

The Last Moment

A sudden outburst of the sun,
Death bells sounded for me to run;
Frighten with despair,
There must be a God somewhere!

A glow of heat that blazed so bright,
So plain to see in my eyesight;
I fled to the rocks to hide my body,
No relief there, oh lordy-lordy!

Rushed to the mountain, the mountain skipped,
Speeding like a powerful ship;
Fire engines gathered to put out the flame,
But oh Lord the world's insane.

As I stopped to catch my breath,
I realize I was seeing death;
The heat was drawing near,
So close, my God it's here!

My legs trembled to run further,
Hoping dear God to find my mother;
A drop of sweat fell from my forehead,
The tormenting fire was tearing me to shreds!

My energy is giving way,
Somebody help me to pray;
The river is steaming and boiling,
That blooded sun is almost falling!

Water, water I must drink,
Before this blazing earth sinks,
The trees that were, are gone,
Merciful Father, I can't last too long.

Forgive me of my sins,
Before this world ends;
The birds have fallen from the sky;
Oh hear me God, "am I going to die?"

Give me eternal life,
Dear God I ask you twice,
End with a consent,
Bring peace at this moment.

Forgetting

Forgetting is a cleansing current,
That washes the clutter from the mind,
From the mole hill to the mountain,
The unpleasant memories it will find.

On the levee of the mind,
Life's dreams and hopes are preserved,
As the currents rushes through,
Clearing the basin of the mind.

The river of knowledge expands the memory,
As the continuous current flows inward,
Before replenishing the tidal basin,
The forgetting tide must flow.

With the birth of the spring season,
Comes the melting of the snow,
The water flows from the mountains,
Creating a current that flows,
Never ending, but onward through time it goes.

Life

Life is reality and filled with
Broken promises.
Life is making and correcting mistakes.
Life is living and loving.
Life is a challenge,
Overcome by the strong.
Life holds truths and
Some spoken words of happiness.
A Life creates new births,
And the weaning of the young.
Life is down-to-earth,
Sunny and stormy, rainy and calm.
Our lives have meaning and
Dedicated toward achieving goals.
When lies are few and childish habits cease,
Love grows,
When all these… and more are met,
Life is beautiful.

Confessions For The Soul

God, my heart is open unto you,
Prepare it Lord.
Plow up the stony ground,
Remove the stumps, rocks, weeds, and debris,
And make it ready for the pure seeds.

Send the Holy Spirit to build a fence
Around my heart to keep out predators.
Then plant the seeds of your word
In the fertile soil of my heart,
And water it with faith, experiences, and wisdom.

Allow the Holy Spirit to walk the landscape of
my heart,
And when He finds roots of bitterness, hatred, greed,
Covetousness, jealousy, selfishness springing up,
Uproot it immediately.

Dear Lord, send the sun to shine upon the seeds,
And let showers of blessing flow from heaven.
Holy Spirit, nurture and protect the seeds
Of God's Holy Word in my heart,
As the plant comes forth fully grown,
Healthy and strong, and producing good fruit.

Won By One

When sin entered the world,
It caused the fall of man,
Sickness, destruction, and death abound,
And temptation lurked on every hand.

Our God was greatly grieved,
Of man's sinful state.
So He sent His only son,
To rescue man's descending fate.

A spotless lamb who knew no sin,
To earth he came to accomplish his Father's mission,
To defeat Satan was His quest,
To conquer death, hell, the grave, and nothing less.

In man's place God offered His son,
To pay the debt for what man had done.
As a babe he came and grew,
And lived among men, women, and children too.

To preach the gospel and heal the sick,
And to set at liberty the bound real quick,
When the time had come to bear His cross,
The disciples and His mom mourned a great loss.

The work is finished, Jesus proclaimed,
From earth He left and ascended in heaven,
With all power in His Holy name.
Then to earth the Father sent,
The Holy Spirit to take His place.

With his sins forgiven, then man,
Re-united with God once again.
And when man look to the Son and believe,
Salvation and eternal life he will receive.

Honey, There Ain't Nothing
Like Church

Honey, there ain't nothing like church,
When good gospel music flows through
The worship place;
And when those choir members' angelic
Voices sing those heavenly songs!
And OH HOW MAJESTIC RING THOSE
GOLDEN SOUNDS BURSTING from the organ!
Can't you hear the rhythmic beating
Of the drums?
And see those liturgical dancers
Electrify the crowd with
UPLIFTED HANDS and PRANCING FEET?
Honey, there ain't nothing like church!

Now watch those folks ALL adorned,
In African prints and kinte strips,
Marching soldierly to the Temple,
And don't you miss those blessed prayers,
Cause they will wash away your sins!
And honey listen to how the saints
Of God rejoice as they fill the offering
Baskets with their tithes and offerings.
And listen to the thunderous pastor's voice,
Beckoning them to "get on board
Little children, get on board!"
And when those young ones
Get redeemed and saved,
Watch those love ones jump and shout!
Honey, there ain't nothing like church!

The Loss of a Coat or Character

In the day of adversity, you will be confronted with
temptation,
When you've been elevated to a position of authority
in this world,
The tempter will surely come to turn your heart
from God.

What will you gain or suffer loss?
Will it be your soul for the riches of this world?
Will it be to gain or keep a position of authority
And lose a godly character?

Joseph suffered the loss of a coat but not character.
When the tempter comes to delete the words
"in God we trust"
From your manna, will your trust be removed
from God
To lotto and casino gambling?

When the accuser comes to afflict the innocent,
Will you suffer righteous persecution,
Or allow the innocent to suffer at the hands of
the ungodly?

Your day of adversity will surely come,
And when it comes, will you suffer the loss
of integrity
To seek a job promotion?

Or will you forsake truth for a lie,
For fear of losing friendships?
Will you suffer the loss of dignity or morality
To seek the pleasures found in sin?

You cannot escape temptation,
For it will come to you and me,
So what will your story be,
The loss of a coat or character?

Love

Love   L-O-V-E
A mother's love,
Calms a child's fears
And rocks him to sleep
Night after night.

Sacrificial love seen in a father
Who provides for his family year after year.
Love – the lifeline of humanity
And the most powerful emotion
Expressed by mankind.

Agape love – Heavenly love,
The only love that comes
From the Father above.

Committed love,
Demonstrated in an elderly couple
Whose love has withstood
The test of time.

Love binds family ties
And bridges the past to the present
And provides a compass to the future.

Love crosses racial lines,
Seeks to understand
And accepts cultural differences,
Love even erases class lines.

Love is seen in a smile,
Felt in a touch,
Gives life to the dying,
Eyes to the blind,
And hope to the hopeless.

Love can mend a broken heart,
Turn a house into a home,
Give a motherless child a baby,
And a homeless child a mother,
Life is worthless without love.

Love blesses, forgives, respects, heals,
Gives, a language of the heart, colorless,
Ageless, a light,
Love L-O-V-E

I Am An Orchestral Praise

My eyes are lifted up toward the heavens and toward
the Almighty who has given
Me sight to see His glory, and wiped away my tears,
I will praise thee.

The Lord has caused my feet to be immoveable and
placed them on the solid rock,
And they will dance in praise unto thee.

Because the Lord has given unto me a mind that is
sound and wavers not.
Oh yes, I will praise thee.

The Lord has harkened unto me and heard my prayers,
And I bow my knees in honor and adoration to thee.

My hands long to praise my God because when
I was bound,
He liberated and came along and set me free,
Oh yes, I will lift both hands and praise thee.

When I prayed unto my God, He gave me a clean
heart and a new spirit,
And filled me with thy power divine,
And now with my whole heart and my spirit,
I will praise thee.

When I stumbled and fell,
He came along and picked me up.
He is my helper and my keeper,
And I will glorify His Holy name.

When the adversary and my enemies came up
against me,
With His mighty hand and outstretched arms,
He delivered me,
Oh yes, I will praise thee.

 When I was cast down and felt all alone,
He touched me with a finger of His love,
Put a smile on my face and lifted up my head,
And I will forever love and adore thee.

And because God has put a new song in my mouth,
And the highest praise upon my lips,
I will glorify and sing all praises to His Holy name.

With my whole body and my life,
I will offer unto my God an orchestral praise,
Glory, glory, glory Hallelujah!

Can I Take Your Reservation, Please? Heaven or Hell

God created us to live forever,
So where do you plan to spend eternity?
Every human being was created by God,
And put within us a free will,
The ability to choose right or wrong,
To make wise or foolish decisions,
To choose life or death.
So, when your earthly life ends,
Where is your reservation?

We have an opportunity while we live on Earth,
To choose Christ and to make Him our Savior.
Yet, some of us reject Him,
And decide to put our trust in some other name.
If you choose to live your life apart from God,
You will be separated from Him in life after death,
For Jesus will say to you on judgment day,
"Depart from me I never knew you."

The truth is, God doesn't consign you to hell,
He only confirms the choice you made.
You may be wondering why doesn't God make
the choice?
Because He didn't create you to be a robot.
From conception, you were given a mind and a
human spirit,
Salvation comes to those who believe in Jesus Christ,

We call upon His Name and everlasting life is
our reward,
And our place is reserved in paradise called heaven.
So, can I take your reservation, please?
Will it be Heaven or Hell?

Just Call Me
Our Father In Jesus' Name

"Winter, spring, summer or fall, no matter what season
Just call, and I'll be there, 'cause you've got
a friend in me,"
Is a song that my friend is singing to you and me.
So listen to the words that's he's singing to us in,
Just call me.

As seasons change, they usher in a change in
the weather.
When the storms of life come and you need a
spring break,
Just call me, and I'll be there, 'cause you've got
a friend.
When the blizzards come, heaping coldness and
a longing
In your heart, and you need some joy in your life,
Just call me, and I'll be there.

When your autumn days come and lingers,
And even your best efforts and intentions fail,
And you look around and see loved ones and friends
Stumbling and falling; disappointment, failure, sorrow,
and defeat,
Are colors in view in your world,
Just call me, and I'll be there to bring the season
of summer
In your life and restore lost joy and laughter,
So you can dance and sing throughout the
winter season.

Just call me, I'm just a prayer away, I'll be there
To calm the raging storm and replace it with peace
in your life.
I'll sow seeds of the word in your life and give
you patience
To await the harvest of blessings to come.
I'll help you to become like a child who finds joy
in every season.
Just call me, and I'll be there in a hurry,
To give you encouragement, and lift your spirit.

I'll be there to replace defeat with victory,
And place your feet on The Solid Rock and
stable ground.
"Winter, spring, summer or fall, no matter
what season
Just call, 'cause you've got a friend in me,"
Just call me, I'm only a prayer away.

Trophies of His Grace

All of mankind and the human race,
Are trophies of God's grace.
Jesus paid the price for sinners,
So we could live our lives as winners.

We feast daily on the living bread,
As the Holy Spirit leads us along the path of truth,
From season to season, we develop our faith,
And grow in the wisdom and knowledge of God.

He gives us experiences and tests in life,
So that spiritual fruit are produced and seen in us.
We pray to the father morning, noon, and night,
Thanking Him for each and every blessing,
As we walk in the holy light.

We serve each other in His presence,
Loving and caring for one another, life's essence,
Until we go home to glory, a heavenly place,
We delight in being trophies of His mighty grace.

Wandered Off...Cry Out

As a child, I wandered away from mom,
In stores, parks, and other places.
Happily moving around and going my way,
Then one fateful day, there appeared no mom in sight.
In desperation I cried out, then suddenly appeared,
My mom with arms out stretched to comfort me.
So secure in her presence I felt,
Walking beside her and holding her loving hand.

Now years have come and gone,
And children I have of my own.
I've watched them become distracted and wander
far from me,
In stores, parks, and other places.
But in desperation, they cried out for me,
Quickly I came with arms out stretched,
To comfort and assure that I was near.
Beside them I walked, holding their tiny hands.

The season came when I left the comfort of home.
My thoughts have wandered and my feet have
taken me
To far and distance places.
But to the Master I cried and quickly He came,
To reveal His presence and comforted me.
So too will the children grow up and leave the
comfort of home.
Temptations and distractions will enter their
thoughts and
Whose feet will cause them to wander off in

distance places.
But when in desperation they cry to the Master,
He will hear and quickly come,
With arms out stretched to bring comfort to their
troubled souls.

My friend, as you read this poem, whether young
or old,
When in life you wander off from the Master,
In stores, parks, and other places.
And you feel so lost and all alone.
Cry out in desperation and He will hear,
And speedily come with arms out stretched,
To comfort and assure that you're not alone.
Rest assured, He's right beside you,
To comfort and assure that you're not alone.

We Are Kingdom Seekers

We are kingdom seekers, seeking the kingdom of God.
We store up the word of God in our hearts,
As we begin this journey of life.
And the word, the heavenly light shines by day
and night
To make our pathway bright.

The road of life is long, narrow, and winding,
Stretching all the way to heaven.
No need to worry about losing our way,
'Cause the word, our compass, directs us on
our journey,
Giving meaning to every road sign.

We are kingdom seekers, unafraid of terror by night,
Or destruction that awaits us at mid-day.
Our God created this world and controls all there
is in it.
The road of life leads us near still water – restoring
our souls.

When the sun beams overhead, and the heat
overtakes us,
God stretches forth his right hand as a shade for us,
We are kingdom seekers journeying on the road,
That will lead us to the promised land.

And as we travel along the way, God's Holy Angels,
Our safety patrols, are stationed at intersections,
So do not fear the thief or robbers who have

Set themselves round about to attack us.

For we are kingdom seekers,
Traveling on the righteous road,
Refueling at every major rest stop of life,
To seek rest for our weary souls,
And nourishment for our weak bodies,
As we travel on this road
That leads us to our heavenly home.

When Jesus Speaks, Listen

I love to read the old testaments books of the Bible,
They tell of what God did from the beginning of time;
The move of God was visible in the lives of Abraham,
Samuel, David, Moses, Isaiah, and many other
Righteous ones who lived during the
Old Testament times.

I read how God brought His children out of Egypt
And delivered them out of the hands of Pharaoh;
I saw how God chose and prepared David for kingship,
How the anointing of the prophet Elijah was passed
onto Elisha.
I even read how Moses mentored Joshua for future
leadership.

But oh how I praise God for what's revealed in the
New Testament books of the Bible, and for what He's
Doing for you and me in the New Testament times.
I get to read the words that Jesus spoke long ago.
As I read the book of Matthew, it is as though I'm
Sitting at the feet of Jesus as He's teaching these
words.

Then my fingers carried me to the book of
Mark, Luke,
And John and I sit for hours reading how Jesus taught
The disciples as the people gathered around.
It is as though Jesus is preparing me as one of His
Disciples as I am transfixed upon His words that
Brings me into His presence.

The truth of Jesus' words fill my heart and soul,
As He speaks uninterrupted in Matthew 6 and 25.
And when He speaks, I still my soul and body
to listen.
And oh what peace, joy, love, and power that flood
my soul.
I've come to understand why Jesus will not take
That which Mary had gained away from her.

When Jesus speaks, cease from labor and striving.
When my Jesus speaks, give Him your undivided
attention.
Read the written words that is printed in red throughout
The New Testament books of the Bible.
When Jesus speaks, there's no need for an interpreter,
'Cause the Holy Spirit is available to give you
understanding.
So fill your heart with the word of God and when
Jesus speaks,
Let it drown out every other voice so you can
listen and hear
Him speak to you.

The Human Spirit

The word of God said, "And the Lord God formed man out of the dust of the
Ground, and breathed into his nostrils the breath of life, and man became
A living soul." (Genesis 2v7) God placed within man a human spirit and man
Began to live and move upon the face of the earth. "Then God gave man
Dominion to rule over every living thing that moveth upon the earth." (Genesis 1v28)

God put within man a free will and this free will gives man the ability to
Choose between good and evil. The human spirit can choose to obey or
Disobey God. God did not leave the human spirit alone, instead, He sent
The Holy Spirit down from heaven to come live and dwell within the
Human body.

God sent the Holy Spirit to the human spirit as its teacher, comforter, and helper.
Its mission is to lead and guide the human spirit into all truth. But it is up to the
Human spirit to follow and be guided by the spirit of truth or be led by the spirit of error.

Down through the ages, the human spirit has been free to listen to the voice of
God or to the voice of Satan. God knew that the human spirit would not always
Choose good over evil, so He sent His son Jesus Christ to pay the sin debt
On its behalf. So when it chooses evil over good and repents, God will forgive
The human spirit and it can return to following the leading of the Holy Spirit.

The human spirit is free to be guided in the light by the Holy Spirit which
Will lead it to eternal life and back to God. But if it chooses to follow the spirit of error and doesn't heed the warning of the spirit of light, it will be led into eternal darkness and thus separated forever from God, the Creator of the human spirit.

A Christian- A Kingdom Kid

A Christian is one who has accepted Jesus Christ
as Savior,
And strives to live a life of faith without a waver.
For he knows that he's joint heirs with Jesus Christ,
Having authority over Satan and dominion on earth
to live a winner's life.

The Holy Spirit, his helper, abides within,
As he walks in divine power and truth, choosing
freedom and liberty,
Instead of bondage and enslavement to sins,
And surrendering his will to the God of love,
To do the will of his Heavenly Father above.

So he fixes and focuses his eyes on Christ,
As he goes through the tests and trials of life,
Realizing that all things work together for good,
Because God, the Father, said they would.

His mind renewed daily in God's Holy Word,
So that he can be the salt and light on earth,
Developing and producing fruit as the spirit birth,
And praying ceaselessly to the Father above,
So his prayers unhindered can be heard.

He clothes himself in armor for warfare,
And join forces with other soldiers to defeat
Satan's strategy,
To kill, steal, and destroy his life with tragedy,

As he faithfully works and journeys through life
with care.

He uses his talents and spiritual gifts to minister
to others,
To fulfill God's will while serving on earth his sisters
and brothers.
Remembering that he was raised up with Christ in
heavenly places
And given all spiritual blessings as an expression of
His grace.

His spirit is guided in God's anointed word each step,
Making him a victor and a conqueror in a life
well kept,
Until his voice is silenced, bodily activity cease, and
the spirit has left,
And entered into his heavenly home in glory,
Leaving behind good works and a blessed life with
a story.

A Priceless Gift For Christmas

What gift can you or I give that is of lasting value?
Give a smile, it sheds light and releases hope into a troubled soul.
Give a hug to a love one, it warms the heart and lifts the spirit.
Comfort a crying child, it calms and quiet his/her fears.
Lend a listening ear, it helps to ease the load someone is carrying.
Visit a grandparent, it is time well spent.
Reach out and mend broken relationships, and await a new beginning.
Read the Christmas Story to a group of preschoolers and spread the true meaning of Christmas.
Make a personal card to give to someone, the loving touch is a welcomed return.
Purchase a book to give to a fatherless child, knowledge elevates the mind.
Contribute to an Angel Tree Project in your community, you are the answer to some child's prayer.
Serenade a sick child in the hospital, it is medicine for the heart and soul.
Engage children in writing letters to families who have lost loved ones due to illnesses, tragic killings, accidents, wars, and hurricanes.
Let's fill young hearts with compassion and love and leave no space for violence and hate.
Visit a nursing home, the seniors will be surprisingly joyful.
Take a picture of a mail carrier and add a note of

appreciation to it.

Give a fruit basket to the sanitation workers, the gift of health is to be greatly valued.

Spend a moment of silence this holiday season to ask for restored peace around the world, the returns will be great in your life.

Team up with a church to assist the homeless and you will learn the meaning of "there was no room in the inn."(Luke 2v7)

These gifts are priceless and have a lasting value.

The Greater Sin

Which sin is greater, betrayal or denial?
Judas turned Jesus over to His enemies,
And thus betrayed the living Christ our Savior.
When confronted in a crowd of persecutors,
Peter denied ever knowing Him.

Was monetary gain Judas' motive for following Jesus?
Is it not profitable today for Church-goers to
follow Christ?
Whether close or afar, they follow and then for reasons,
untold,
Turn away too.
What about compromising Christians, who go along,
keep silent,
Or are indifferent to righteousness to avoid
persecution?
They deny Christ by the lives they live,
And for not taking a stand for righteousness in
this world.

Betrayal or denial, which is the greater sin?
The spotlight is shining upon both disciples who
walked with Christ.
Peter acknowledged his sin and repented to the heav-
enly Father.
And God stepped in, forgave him, and washed away
his sin.
Peter's soul reflected upon Jesus' teachings and he
took Christ at His Word.

Now Judas was sorrowful and perhaps wept over
his sin,
But he allowed his accusing conscience to condemn
him,
Thus, he turned and departed from the living Christ.
The bible said that he repented to the chief priests
and Jewish leaders,
But what about confessing his repentance to God
and receive an instant
Pardon? Mat. 27v3,4, 1John 1v9)
Judas' soul did not reflect upon the truth of
Christ coming
Into the world to pay mankind's sin debt and the
death penalty,
And that included the sin of betrayal, but reflected
instead upon his sin,(Ps.51v3,4)
Hence, God could not move on Judas' behalf.
Did Judas die with a change of mind but without
an unrepentance's
Heart?

Is the sin of betrayal greater than the sin of denial?
Peter wept bitterly over his sin, repented, forgave
himself, and returned to Christ.
He had a change of heart and went forth to fulfill
his ministry
Of teaching and preaching repentance and remission
of sins,
Which is the Gospel of Jesus Christ.
Judas had deep regrets and was sorrowful but turned
away from Christ.
Did he die in his sins with a changeless heart?

And with unforgiveness directed toward himself?
His life came to an abrupt end and he was unable
To fulfill God's call and plan for his life.
Oh, if only he had repented and allowed God
to forgive
The sin of betrayal, he too could have gone forth
To share the good news of the Gospel of Jesus Christ,
And put an end to this age old question of,
Which is the greater sin?

On Trial In The World's Courtroom

What is your name?
A Christian my lord.
What is your name?
A Christian my lord.

Who are you?
A witness for Christ my lord.
Who are you?
A witness for Christ my lord.

What do you confess?
That Jesus is the son of God my lord.
What do you confess?
That Jesus is the son of God my lord.

What is your crime?
I'm a follower of the Lord Jesus Christ my lord.
What is your crime?
I'm a follower of the Lord Jesus Christ my lord.

You are sentenced to a life of persecution, trials, and
tribulations.
Then so be it my lord,
Then so be it my lord.

Spiritual Bees

When a life is governed by its rules and selfish will,
It attracts distress,
And chases away divine peace and sweet rest.

When a life seeks after worldly ambition and
worldly gain,
It opens the door and leaves an entrance to
limitless pain,
For which you cannot restrain.

When a life looks to man for advice and counsel
for life's direction,
You are moving away from the Holy Spirit's
protection,
Because my God gives clear instructions and
directions.
And now I offer you my godly conclusion,
A believer who will live a life of confusion.

These are the spiritual bees that will come and abide,
And build their hives and combs in your earthly
home,
Until you surrender your will and allow the
Holy Spirit to be your guide.

Wash My Feet, Lord

Wash my feet Lord
Wash my feet,
 Yes Lord, wash away the stain and the pain of sin.

As I journey through this world of sin,
My feet gathers dust and dirt
And it's visible to you Lord within;
So Lord, I need you to wash my feet,
Lord, wash my feet,
Wash away the stain and the pain of sin.

These feet tread and trod
Through communities and distant places,
Shedding and spreading light
And the gospel of peace,
And they become tired, swollen, and in pain.

As I make my way to your throne of grace,
At the close of each day that I've faced,

To pull off my shoes to rest my weary and worn feet
In a holy and a peaceful place,
Asking you Lord to wash my feet,
Lord, wash my feet,
Wash away the stain and the pain of sin.

A Yes Prayer

Dear Father, the family is in disarray,
I've looked and waited for you to appoint someone,
To fulfill his or her rightful place as a servant in
this ministry;
But the Holy Spirit just won't leave me alone.
So Lord, I surrender my will to you, and my heart
Gives you a YES and an AMEN;
I shall arise and go forth,
Take all of me and use me for Your Glory,
In the Mighty Name of Jesus Christ I pray.

A Christian Family Constitution

We will love God with all our hearts, souls, strength, and obey his commandments. (Mat.22v37)

We will commit to the Lordship of Jesus Christ.

We will honor God with our bodies.

We will love, support, encourage, and respect one another. We will promote a nurturing family Environment.

We will allow the word of God to be the standard for our lives and in our home.

We will strive to build a strong Christian family.

We will pray together as a family.

We will listen to and communicate effectively with each other.

We will implement a good work ethic in our home, hold family discussions, and make family decisions together.

We will promote positive conduct and behaviors among family members and others.

We will attend a local church together and become active members.

We will function as a family team and promote the spirit of cooperation.

We will nurture each family members' individuality and uniqueness.

We will make our home our primary biblical training, teaching, and worship center.

We will strive to live a healthy, disciplined, and balanced life.

We will eat nutritious meals together, promote, and support family physical fitness.

We will seek wholesome entertainment and recreational activities and fellowship together.

We will take family vacations together.

We will learn how to manage our money.

We will educate ourselves about the difference between creationism and evolution.

We will develop a Christian worldview.

We will educate ourselves about the media and technology, pledge to honor

God in our media choices, and make proper use of technology.

We will educate ourselves about the political system and understand how it operates.

A Godly Home

A godly home is a place where you learn about God and cultivate godliness.

A home is where a family grows spiritually, work, play, and fellowship together. The home on earth is to pattern after and reflects the household of God. Daily family worship and devotion take place in a godly home.

A godly home is a place where God's divine order is carried out. The father is the head of the family and the mother is the heart of the family. It is place of security and stability.

Christ is the head of a godly home.

A godly home is where a godly family is built. It is the place where the husband /wife, father/mother and parent/child relationships are developed. Godly children are raised, taught, and trained.

The home is where children learn to obey God's commandments, obey, and respect authority. Godly boundaries and standards are set and enforced. The Ten Commandments and the Lord's Prayer are visible in the home.

A godly home has an atmosphere of love, peace, and the presence of God. Children can see godly examples in their parents as they are taught in the ways of the Lord.

A godly home is covered with the covering of prayer. It is a place where hospitality dwells.

A godly home is where the family learns faith, honor, respect, trust, commitment, obedience, service, sharing, and caring.

A home is the place where servants' hearts and fruitful lives are developed.

A godly home should contain spiritual and educational resources, and other edifying materials and resources.

A home is the place where visions are nurtured and effective communication

And fellowship flourishes. It is a place where the family learns to listen to each other and to the voice of God.

A godly home is structured and organized.

A Godly Marriage

A marriage is a spiritual covenant between God,
a man and a woman who share their lives together.

A marriage is designed for the glory of God and allows
Him to reveal His love through mankind.

In a godly marriage, the couple dedicates and gives
himself and herself to each other and to God.

A godly marriage is built upon the word of God, guided
by the Holy Spirit, and lay claims to the promises of
God.

In a godly marriage, both the husband and wife are
believers in God and will strive to achieve oneness
in their marriage and oneness in Christ. The image of
Christ is revealed in the husband and the wife.

A marriage allows a husband and a wife to grow in
their knowledge and understanding (personality and
needs) of each other. The couple learns to listen and
communicate effectively with each other.

In a marriage, a couple learns to be subject to one
another and walk in a spirit of humility, godly attitude,
and obedience to God.

A marriage is the relationship between God, the couple, the families, and a connection to the future generations.

A marriage is the foundation upon which the family is built. Prayer and godly characters will help preserve and sustain the relationship.

In a marriage, the husband and wife grow together in compatibility as each develop his/her gifts and retain his/her uniqueness. A nurturing environment is created to allow visions and creativity to flourish. The husband and wife complement each other.

In a godly marriage, the couple prays and have family devotion together, and plan for their future family according to their understanding of God's will for them.

The marriage union is a place for fruitfulness and procreation. The couple dines together.

In a godly marriage, the couple will produce the fruit of the Holy Spirit in their lives.

A marriage is built upon mutual trust and account-ability, loyalty, fidelity, and a holy standard of morality.

In a godly marriage, the couple must have unwavering faith in God to stand when the seasons of adversity comes. They must sow seeds of appreciation, compliment and praise, respect, care and concern, courtesy, compassion, kindness, contentment, encouragement, and build each other up in the faith. They embrace, hug, and bless each other in thoughts, words, and deeds.

In a marriage, the couple must love unconditionally, cover faults with prayer, walk in forgiveness, reconciliation, restoration, compromise, and mutual agreement.

In a godly marriage, the couple walks in unity (spirit, soul, and body), harmony, and maturity. They are united in a bond of friendship, commitment, shared responsibilities and financial resources, cooperation, generosity, and mutual values.

They plan their family together, support career endeavors, share common interests, recreational activities and entertainment. They enjoy wholesome conversation, fellowship, and discuss world news from a Christian worldview.

In a marriage, the couple strives to live a balance life and manage their time wisely.

A Godly Husband

A godly husband loves God with all his heart, soul, and strength, and obeys His Commandments. (Mat. 22v37)

A godly husband makes Christ the Lord of his life, the center of his marriage, and submit to the Lordship of Christ.

A godly husband will seek God's will and divine purpose for his life. He has a vision for his marriage, family, and for himself.

A godly husband is the spiritual leader and the head of his home and family.

A godly husband will be of the same mind and unified in the spirit with his godly wife.

A godly husband loves, honors, and respects his wife.

A godly husband manages the family financial resources and strives to be debt free.

A godly husband makes decisions based upon godly wisdom and the Holy Spirit's guidance.

A godly husband understands that his wife thinks differently and ask God to help them both to see things from His perspective.

A godly husband realizes that he should always pray for his wife and with his wife even though he might not understand her.

A godly husband blesses his wife with his thoughts, words, and deeds.

A godly husband spends time, listens, communicates effectively, and develops a holy relationship with his wife.

A godly husband will strive to keep romance in his marriage.

A godly husband will accept his wife as his teammate.

A godly husband will ask God to show him how his wife compliments him.

A godly husband is trustworthy.

A Godly Wife

A godly wife loves God with all her heart, soul, and strength, and obeys His commandments. (Mat. 22v37)

A godly wife is a virtuous woman.

A godly wife honors the covenant that was made with God and her husband.

A godly wife loves, respects, and honors her husband.

A godly wife is unified in the spirit and joined together in the same mind as her godly husband.

A godly wife will submit to a godly husband as he is in submission to God.

A godly wife sees her husband through God's eyes.

A godly wife base her worth not on affirmation from the world and its images,

But on the word of God.

A godly wife is the heart of the home. She builds her home and makes it a sanctuary for her family.

A godly wife has a vision for her marriage, family, and for herself.

A godly wife prays that God will keep the marriage intact and build a strong marriage. She prays with her godly husband and before she speaks and acts.

A godly wife has a gentle and quiet spirit. She reflects the Lord's beauty.

A godly wife spends quality time with her husband to build a holy relationship.

A godly wife communicates effectively with her husband and comes to mutual agreements and compromises.

A godly wife manages the family financial resources together with her husband.

A godly wife is a teammate to her husband and is committed to working together.

A godly wife is a blessing and a gift from God.

A Godly Daughter

A godly daughter loves, trust, and obeys the commandments of God.

A godly daughter listens to and obeys the instructions of her father and mother.

A godly daughter submits to the authority of her father and mother. She willingly accepts and obeys the rules and boundaries that her parents have set for her and the home.

A godly daughter prays for her parents and siblings.

A godly daughter looks to her godly mother as her godly model and teacher. She opens her heart to her mom as she counsels and prays for her. She learns from her godly mother and other godly mothers her role as a fruit carrier, nurturer, and home builder.

A godly daughter honors and respects her parents.

A godly daughter will fellowship with her family on The Sabbath or Sunday. She loves and obeys the Word of God.

A godly daughter spends time in devotion and prayer with her family.

A godly daughter has a teachable and humble spirit. She also has a gentle and quiet spirit. She learns to submit and obey authority.

A godly daughter has a loving relationship with her family members.

A godly daughter understands that abstinence is God's plan for her until

Marriage. A godly daughter learns from other godly women the importance of keeping the temple (the body) holy and clean.

A godly daughter has inner beauty that radiates outwardly. She dresses in modest apparel.

A godly daughter loves, respects, forgives, helps, and cares for her siblings.

A godly daughter, like a wise virgin, plans, and prepares to achieve a first rate education. She takes advantage of the opportunities that are available to her.

A godly daughter develops her faith walk with her Heavenly Father.

A godly daughter learns to listen and communicate effectively with her family members.

A Godly Son

A godly son loves God with all his heart, soul, and strength, and obeys His Commandments. (Mat. 22v37)

A godly son will put his faith and trust in God and will continue to grow into a strong godly man.

A godly son learns from his godly father and other godly men his role as a leader, protector, and a provider.

A godly son will listen and obey the wise counsel and instruction of his father and mother.

A godly son will willingly receive wisdom, knowledge, and instruction from his parents.

A godly son will recognize, as he matures, Christ in his godly father's life.

A godly son, looks to his godly father to mentor and guide him into manhood.

A godly son develops a good relationship with his dad. He inherits and passes on his father's name. He learns to listen and communicate effectively with his dad.

A godly son learns the work ethics from his godly father.

A godly son comes to understand, through godly men, the character of a godly man. He learns how to respect, honor, and treat his mother, sister, and other women.

A godly son prays for and with his father, mother, and siblings.

A godly son will accept chastisement and correction from his father and mother. He learns how to respect and obey authority.

A godly son learns the value of a good name, godly character, and integrity. He learns to do right instead of wrong.

A godly son trains his eyes where to look and what to focus upon. He understands that abstinence is God's plan until marriage. He learns from other godly men the importance of keeping the temple (the body) holy and clean.

A godly son allows his godly father to guide him into the world as he learns about it and its political system. He learns to become a man of peace instead of a man of war.

A godly son leans upon God, his Heavenly Father, as he matures into manhood, and less upon his earthly father.

A Father's Commandments

Be obedient to God's commandments and hold God's word as the standard and the authority for your life and the life of your family.

Be a godly role model and have Christ as the center of your life and model your faith in God to your family. Model a godly healthy and loving husband/wife relationship in the home. (consult spiritual and professional experts)

Build a strong Christian family and home. Provide a nurturing environment for your children. Lead by love and self-sacrifice.

Love your wife and children and show respect toward them.

Listen to and build good communication with your children. (consult spiritual and professional experts)

Set a standard rule of your family eating meals together.

Develop a strong parent relationship with your children. (consult spiritual and professional experts)

Provide for, protect, and be a good steward over your family.

Hold daily devotional, prayer, and family counsel with your family. Teach your family how to work, pray, serve, and play together.

(consult spiritual and professional experts)

Seek wisdom from God and walk in it.

Set godly boundaries and standards and enforce them in your home.

Discipline your children in love.

Teach and train your children in the ways of the Lord.

Take your children to a Christ-centered, bible teaching local church and become active members.

Teach your children the biblical worldview and educate them about the media, technology, politics, and the world. (consult spiritual and professional experts)

Enforce a modest apparel and appearance in the home. (The human body is not the place to display art form).

Teach the children to think critically, discern, and allow them to be a part of the decision-making team.

Teach the children the truth in God's word and right from wrong.

Spend quality time with your children and take them with you.

Teach your children how to manage their money and to be responsible. (consult spiritual and professional experts)

Seek out other godly families to enjoy fellowship with and participate in recreational activities.

Provide wholesome entertainment and recreational activities for your family. Take your family on vacations.

Educate your children about courtship and dating. (consult spiritual and professional experts)

Read to and encourage children to read classic literature and listen to spiritual and inspirational music.

Choose wisely the educational system for your child(ren) and become an active member of the educational team.

A Mother's Commandments

Love God with all your heart, soul, and strength, and keep His Commandments. (Mat.22v37)

Love and honor your husband.

Encourage and pray for your husband to be the spiritual leader in the home.

Be a godly example for your child(ren).

Raise your child(ren) in a godly home.

Train and teach your child(ren) in the ways of the Lord.

Assist God in developing a godly character in your child(ren).

Develop a prayer life and pray prevailing prayers for your family.

Be devoted to reading God's word daily, listen to spiritual and inspirational music in the home, and pray with your child(ren).

Seek wisdom from God and walk in it.

Love, hug, and use appropriate discipline to chasten your child(ren).

Bless your child(ren) with your words.

Reinforce the boundaries and standards of the home.

Provide for and protect your child(ren).

Listen and communicate with your child(ren).

Enforce the standards and rules of the family eating meals together.

Establish and maintain a strong parent relationship with your child(ren).

Provide godly advice and counsel to your child(ren).

Spend quality time with your child(ren) in order to catch teachable moments.

Provide your child(ren) with opportunities and real life experiences.

Enjoy clean entertainment and recreational activities with your child(ren).

Teach your child(ren) to love people and value the life of animals and other living things.

Teach your child(ren) to work, be orderly, dependable, and responsible.

Teach your child(ren) how to manage their money (tithe and save).

Locate a Christ-centered Church with your husband for the family.

Develop relationships and fellowship with other godly families.

Educate your child(ren) about the media.

Teach your child(ren) how to think critically and to spiritually discern good from evil.

Cook nutritious meals for your family.

Locate a good medical team to care for the health of the family.

A Child's Commandments

Obey your parents in the Lord, honor, and respect your mother and father. (Eph.6v1,2)

Love God with all of your heart, soul, and might. (Deut. 6v5)

Love yourself and your neighbor. (Mat. 19v19)

Obey those authorities that have been placed above you who guide you in the right way.

Commit your life to God, accept Jesus as your Lord and Savior, and the Holy Spirit as your teacher.

Seek to know and do God's will for your life.

Attend Sunday School, study the bible, memorize bible verses, and learn the Apostle's Creed.

Develop a godly character and attitude. Learn to do what's right instead of wrong.

Learn to pray and pray daily for yourself, family, community, school, country, and its leaders. Pray with your mom, dad, and siblings.

Choose other children who are Christians as your friends.

Stay clear of ungodly images, music, and speech. Monitor what you see on television, at the theatre, on the computer and hear on the radio, CD's, and DVD's.

Develop your God- given gifts and talents.

Eat healthy meals, limit junk food, exercise regularly and get the proper amount of sleep.

Complete your daily chores and responsibilities.

Develop a Christian worldview.

Read classic literature, and listen to spiritual and inspirational music.

A Christian Teen Constitution

Love God with all your heart, soul, and strength. (Mat. 22v37)

Hide the ten (10) commandments in your heart so that you will be victorious in your faith walk.

Obey your parents in the Lord; honor and respect your mother and father. (Eph. 6v1,2)

Respect and obey authority who teaches you what is right.

Learn to do what's right and not what the majority agrees to.

The body is the temple of God, therefore reject drugs and alcohol; maintain sexual purity.

And avoid junk food by eating healthy foods.

Remember and obey the biblically based boundaries that God and your parents have set before you.

Develop your intellect, acquire knowledge, and get a first (1st) rate education.

Develop the ability to think critically and make wise decisions.

Seek godly counsel from your parents, spiritual, and professional experts.

Be up-to-date on world news and develop a Christian worldview.

Develop your faith and attend a bible teaching and believing church.

Pray for godly friends and then look for them involved in church ministries.

Pray for your family, community, church, school, the country, and its leaders.

Understand that all forms of unwholesome entertainment and fellowship will corrupt your character.

Use the WWJD principle when making media choices and in dating situations.

Be modest in your appearance and do not stand in the way of someone who is searching for a better way.

Drive within the speed limits.

Be a light at home, at school, and in the community. Live a disciplined life.

A Young Adult Constitution

Love God with all your heart, soul, and strength; abide by the "thou shalts" in the Ten Commandments.

Honor and respect your parents.

Seek the truth and walk in it.

Develop your faith, values, and morals and strive to live a balanced life.

Walk in honesty, integrity, and sexual purity.

Set your aim to achieve the master's plan for your life.

Strive to become discipline and manage your time.

Pray for a godly mate, godly friends, and keep company with other believers.

Serve your fellowman and live a selfless life.

Pray for your family, community, church, place of work, state, country, the world and its leaders.

Seek godly counsel from your parents, spiritual Leaders, and professional experts,

Manage your finances and fulfill your responsibilities.

Preserve your health by eating healthy food and balanced meals.

Maintain physical fitness.

Get annual physical examinations.

Make decisions based upon biblical principles.

Develop a Christian worldview and keep abreast of world news.

Be a responsible adult driver.

Avoid judging to condemn but judge to evaluate.

Be a light in the world.

A Godly Sister

A godly sister loves God with all her heart, soul, and strength, and obeys His Commandments. (Mat. 22v37)

A godly sister will be found in God's house worshipping and serving with the people of God. You will be able to see Christ in her life.

A godly sister accepts the real you. She will shower you with her love and hugs. She will spend time developing a godly friendship with you.

A godly sister is a trusted friend. You can confide in her and reveal your heart to her. She is learning to listen and communicate with you and her Heavenly Father.

A godly sister is an encourager and a supporter. She brings out the best in you. She is there for you in the good and the bad times.

A godly sister is loving and compassionate. She walks in reconciliation, forgiveness, mercy, grace, and truth.

A godly sister has a gentle and quiet spirit. Her inner beauty radiates outwardly.

A godly sister adorns herself in modest apparel.

A godly sister is one who is growing in wisdom, knowledge, and understanding. She is developing a spirit of discernment.

A godly sister is a praying sister and will lift you up in prayer. She spends time in devotion reading God's word.

A godly sister will bless you with her thoughts, words, and deeds. She will speak the truth to you in love.

A godly sister will cry with you when you are sad and rejoice with you when you are joyful. She will comfort you when you need comforting.

A godly sister will walk together with you on the righteous path and hold you accountable. She realizes that ungodly places, people, and media choices will corrupt a godly character. She strives to walk in holiness.

A Godly Brother

A godly brother loves God with all his heart, soul, and strength, and obeys His commandments. (Mat. 22v37)

A godly brother will be found in God's house worshipping and serving others.

A godly brother is loving and compassionate.

A godly brother spends time reading God's word. He is being transformed into the image of Christ.

A godly brother will strive to walk in holiness. He learns how to read nonverbal body language and body boundaries. He learns how to avoid and stay out of temptation. He learns how to train his eyes where to look and what to focus upon.

A godly brother respects and honors women. A godly brother learns how to identify godly and ungodly characteristics in a woman.

A godly brother learns to develop a spirit of discernment.

A godly brother spends time reading God's word.

A godly brother is one who is growing in wisdom, knowledge, and understanding.

A godly brother is a praying brother. He has a burden for his unsaved brothers and for his saved brothers who are walking in sin.

A godly brother has tough love. He accepts the real you, but challenges you to be God's best. He speaks the truth in love. He will hold you accountable and will be there for you when you stumble and fall.

A godly brother is an encourager and a supporter.

A godly brother walks in a spirit of humility.

A godly brother walks in love, reconciliation, forgiveness, and peace.

A godly brother will be found developing his gifts and abilities and taking advantage of God-given career opportunities.

A godly brother is a masculine brother.

A godly brother is a trusted friend.

What You Gonna Do About It?

The family is being redefined by the unrighteous, and many of our youth are part of gangs.

Aids have reached epidemic proportions among people of color.

The divorce rate in the Christian community is comparable to those in the nonchristian community.

What you gonna do about it?

Quality education for all children in the public schools seem to no longer have a place on the political agenda.

Promoting abstinence over abortion and fornication is not a collective fight of the righteous.

Violence and obscenity are entertainment for our youth today.

What you gonna do about it?

More young men and now young women are entering the prison institution at an alarming rate than into institutions for higher learning.

Unhealthy eating, lifestyles, and poor health are affecting the young and the old.

What you gonna do about it?

Haiti has been raped and the islands have been robed.

Many countries are coveting their neighbors' goods and going to war to possess them.

Africa needs to be restored.

What you gonna do about it?

Technology is widening the gap between the haves and have-nots.

More and more children are raised outside of the homes by community

Care-givers. Many parents carry their children to movie theaters than to museums, zoos, and recreation parks.

What you gonna do about it?

Child abuse and neglect are on the increase.

Many children are raised in single parent homes, and are more knowledgeable about sports, clothes, and movies than science, math, and current events.

What you gonna do about it?

Earth, Our Home

Earth is home for the human race.
Earth is a kingdom for the plants and animals.
It gives us food and shelter.

But earth is becoming endangered.
The land and the seas are polluted by man,
Because man has forgotten how
To take care of home.

The animals run in fear for their lives,
Because they know that man has
Forgotten how to care for and protect them.
Many plants are gone and no more as we knew them.

We, the children, throughout the world,
Must help our parents to see
What they're doing to the home
That we have received.

We must spread the news of the tragic state of home,
And put a stop to this destruction,
Just to make more bucks,
And we must promise to nurture and protect,
The life on earth that the creator has made,
And cherish our home forever.

Water

We need water to live,
It is a fact of life that's real,
But some water is unsafe to drink,
So mankind must come together to plan and think.

Fish and other living creatures need water to live,
But some oceans and seas have oil spills,
And our source of food have been greatly endangered,
So what solution or ideas will come from the ponder?

We need water to bathe and swim,
Some animals and insects do the same thing too.
We rejoice when the Creator sends rain showers
our way,
And the animals and insects welcome the rainy days.

An Invisible Friend

Air

Air warms us and makes us cold.
We can't see it or touch it,
But we can feel it.

Air is as light as a feather,
And when it's strong,
It can knock down trees and homes.

Did you know that air
Is made up of nitrogen and oxygen?
Our earth is full of air,
But the moon is void of air.

Trees and other green plants
Are needed on earth,
Because they put oxygen
Into the air that we breathe.
I'm so glad that earth has an invisible friend!

Earth

E **Eager** to be our earthly home

A The **air** that we breathe each day

R Our home is **rich** and full of plenty

T Take the **time** to keep our home clean and safe

H A **healthy** home is a happy home

Air

You can see through it and feel it,
But you can't taste it or smell it.
Air is everywhere on earth,
But you can't find it on the moon.

You can put it in a balloon,
And put it in a tire.
Air can whistle at you
And even make you dance.

Air can help you take off your hat,
And lift up your hair and skirt.
Plants make the air good for you and me.
I like air, do you?

A Champion Of Faith
(Kenneth E. Hagin)

A Saint who took God at His Word.
Sick and bedridden as a child on a bed of affliction,
And given up by doctors as death crept into his room;
But suddenly, the sword of the spirit was opened
and read,
And his faith was activated and the inner man fed.
Then he arose from his sick bed totally healed
and set free.

Satan's lies and deception were exposed and
demons fled,
As the truth gave life to his sick body and weak soul.
The Holy Spirit, the comforter and teacher, taught
him the bread of life,
Which is His assigned purpose and ultimate goal.
Then he conquered sickness, death, and poverty,
And went on to live a victorious life on earth
in Christ.

The new testament Father of Faith who communed
with God,
And a chosen disciple of the Lord Jesus Christ.
He established a Bible Training School and taught
believers around the world,
How to activate their faith in God's true and living
Word,

And many souls have been redeemed from a life of
sin and bondage,
And have come to know that through Christ's poverty
we've been made rich.

His spirit, soul, and body were preserved,
To fulfill God's work of faith with power,
As God counted him worthy of this calling for
the hour,
He taught us how to watch, pray, and to never cease,
And to receive the love of the truth in our hearts
and minds,
Because God's word will release and set us free.

A humble servant and a true Prophet of God,
Full of the Holy Spirit and mature in his faith.
Pastor Kenneth Hagin helped to strengthen and
build up
The body of Christ and the family of God.
He's now home in glory seated among the elders,
Rejoicing and praising around the Holy Throne
of God.
The mantle is passed along with the baton,
To those of us who are faithful to the call, to teach
truth so others will be won.

Daughter Of Grace

Born in the land of Egypt,
A descendant of earthly kings and queens,
Yet created to do the Master's will.
Flourished and nourished in a kingly palace,
Taken and placed into a dingy pit,
Yet predestined to reign and rule in heavenly
places.

A persecutor of believers in Christ,
A faithful soldier on the Prince of this world's mission
field,
Heard a voice from heaven – Christ the Savior,
Blinded on the broad road of destruction,
Led into the Holy City to receive one's sight from a
disciple of Christ,
Then changed her name to daughter of Grace,
And placed her feet on the street called straight.

Raised and highly favored by pharaoh,
Slew an Egyptian and sent into exile,
Sojourned for a season into the desert and the
wilderness,
Shepherded and took care of her kinsman's flock,
Journeyed to the mountaintop to hear the Father's
voice,
And received the call of God for her life.

Resurrected and raised from the dead,
Replaced the graved clothes with a robe of

righteousness,
Anointed and appointed to be the deliverer,
To fulfill the covenant that God made to Abraham.
Put a staff in her hand and His Holy Word in her
mouth,
And sent back to Egypt to deliver God's children out
of sin and bondage.

Transformed from a Martha – a task oriented
busy body,
Into a Mary – one who delights in praise and
worship.
Anointed as a mighty prayer warrior – an
intercessor like Christ,
Proclaimed as the deliverer by the prophets of old
(Simeon and Anna).
Nike Daramy, an Apostle, a Prophetess, a Pastor,
a teacher, a mentor, a wife, a mother, a daughter, a
daughter-in-law, a sister, a cousin, a godmother, and
a trusted friend.

A Real Hero
(Rev. Dr. Martin Luther King Jr.)

Dr. King was a real hero,
Full of faith, hope, and love,
And even courage too.
He helped make the world a better place for mankind.
He touched the lives of people of many nations,
Exposing evil and encouraging us to stand for
righteousness.
"Fight the spirit of hate with the weapon of love," he
preached.
Dr. King was a real hero.

"We must unite to become a strong and mighty force,
And use our civic power to defeat injustice,"
he would say.
Even the children ceased their play and went to work,
For they knew the season of time we faced.
Dr. King was a prophet of God who proclaimed,
The message of peace across the land.
He was persecuted and cast into jail for leading a
noble cause.
The city and state leaders demonstrated their power,
In hope that fear gripped the hearts of those that
followed The King.
But Dr. King pointed the people to God,
"Trust Him to allow justice and righteousness to
prevail," he said.
Dr. King was a real hero.

Yes, the day came when God let justice prevail in the land, and he took Dr. King from his earthly home,

But left us with hope for tomorrow in the form of a dream that Dr. King shared with us before journeying to his heavenly home.

A dream that has yet to be fulfilled here on earth,

Because God wants us to keep trusting and looking to Him,

To allow justice and righteousness to prevail throughout the land.

Our charge is to pass this hope and dream onto the new generation.

Thank you Dr. King for your work and dedication, And for being a real hero.

Pope John Paul II

A pioneer, a world leader, a lion for peace,
A warrior for social justice and human rights.
Pope John Paul II was a well educated man,
A philosopher, translator, poet, playwright,
and a writer.

Pope John Paul II was an athlete in his youth,
A swimmer, skier, hiker, and one who enjoyed
kayaking.
Throughout his ministry, he opposed abortion,
euthanasia,
Death, penalty, and even excessive capitalism.

Pope John Paul II was a man of faith,
He was acquainted with sickness, pain, and suffering.
Nevertheless, he touched the lives of many people,
And blessed them in a very special way.

Pope John Paul II was Polish and yet,
He reached out to people of many nations and races,
Bringing unity and love and understanding,
And worked to tear down the Iron Curtain in Russia.

Pope John Paul II was laid to rest on April 2, 2005,
Millions of people around the world pilgrimage
to Rome,
To say farewell to this compassionate Roman
Catholic leader.
Although his life has ended, he will long be remem-
bered, as a Saint and Pope John Paul the Great.

Thurgood Marshall

Children, education, law, change, what do these
words have to do with Thurgood Marshall?
Well, let me tell you in a poem,
How this black man gained a victory,
And will forever be remembered in history.

Long ago black and white children,
Couldn't go to school together to learn,
So education for blacks were far from the best.
Thurgood Marshall – a lawyer trained,
Worked and worked to proclaim,
 That America's laws had to change.

He didn't think separate but equal laws were
just and good, so he worked to make his ideas
understood.
Education for whites was indeed superior,
But for blacks, it was by far inferior.

Little Rock Central High was the first to integrate,
But many schools far and near,
Refused to set the record straight.
Yet laws in America had to change,
So schools by law were forced to desegregate.

President Johnson years later,
Appointed Marshall as a U.S. Judge,
And he worked for the people united as one,
Until he retired and his work on earth was done.

So now you know how Thurgood Marshall,
Is connected with children, education, and legal
victory.
Throughout America this is a story to tell,
And he will long be remembered in American
history.

Dr. James Dobson
(Focus on the Family)

A modern day Noah, whose mission
Is to rescue families here on earth.
Born and grew up in a godly home.
Just an ordinary boy, predestined to do extraordinary
things.

Jim became a psychologist who brought healing
Into the lives of children.
Faithful to the call, he filled his day with children,
Until a lovely one caught his eye by the name
of Shirley.
In love they fell, and then married.

The two lived happily, adding more joy and life into
their family.
As the season of time unfolded,
God called Jim to his earthly mission,
Thus began Focus on the Family.

And God blessed Focus on the Family and Jim's
family too.
Like Abraham, Jim had to leave his kinsmen and
journey to another place.
Around the world, families were restored and healed
as well.
Their children grew in a godly family and then
left home,

Then God looked to Shirley to gather the nations
for prayer.

Together, Jim and Shirley ministered to families,
And summoned the nations for prayer.
Now they train others to carry on this heavenly
mission,
Of bringing restoration to families and healing too.
So let it be written in the book of Hebrews,
The faithfulness of Jim Dobson and
Shirley Dobson too.

We Celebrate You
(Dedicated to Marie Clay)

Because of you, generations of youth
Will see and walk into a bright future.

You've empowered teachers to nourish
The dreams they hold in their hearts,
Until they take root and spring forth.

With your life, you've helped to recover
And release children's imaginations to
Fly to faraway places by reading books.

And just like birds in the sky, we sing
While the sun shines upon our lives,
As we soar around the world,
To honor and celebrate you.

Mamma's Hands
(Dedicated to my loving mother)

Mamma's hands carried me and lifted me up in
her lap

As she rocked me to sleep.
They were folded in prayer for me before she tucked
me in bed.
Mamma's hands prepared and cooked meals for me,
And poured medicine in spoons and gave to me.
They washed my dirty face, cleaned my nose, bathed
and clothed me.
They washed and groomed my kinky hair for me.

Mamma's hands loved me, hugged me, and even
chastened
And played with me.
They washed, ironed, and folded clothes for me.
They shopped and brought home sacks of food for me,
And cut stacks of wood to keep our home warm
for me.

Mamma's hands made birthday cakes, cookies,
ice cream,
And lemonade and desserts to celebrate special
days for me.
They cooked meals for the sick and homeless
And for those who had lost love ones.
They planted and toiled gardens to produce food
For her family and that included me.

Mamma's hands held opened hymnals as she sang
Songs of praises and held opened the Holy Bible as
She read God's Word before resting her head on the
Pillar at night.
They echoed claps of joy as she danced and sang
while she did her chores around the house.
They fitted me with shoes and put blankets and quilts
On my bed to keep me warm throughout the wintry
nights.

Mamma's hand held my hands as I took my first steps,
And those same hands walked me across the busy
streets.
I watched mamma's hands grow old as they wore
lines and
Wrinkles, cuts, burns, and bruises.
But they were manicured and polished and kept clean
each day.
They were dressed up in gloves, and held a
tambourine and directed
Church choirs on Sunday mornings.
Mamma's hands were so, so, busy.
But now, mamma's hands are resting and away
from me.
Oh how I miss mamma's hands.
Those hands that were filled with so much love
for me
And so many others.

Those hands that God used to provide for me
And so many others.
Those hands that wrote letters and sent cards to me

And so many others.
Those hands that were lifted up in praise and
prayer for me
And so many others.

Oh how I miss mamma's hands.
Those hands that held me close to her because
God told her to.
Now mamma's hands are home in glory still
lifted high in praise
And in prayer for me
And for so many others.

The One In The Middle
(Cheryl)

The one in the middle,
Whose heart is made of silver and pure gold,
Filled with caring, sharing, compassion, and
treasures untold.
A helper, a giver, a cleaner, and a modern day chef
unfolds.
A character that's reserve, quiet, tender, kindhearted,
and bold.

Precious in her sight is the life of an animal and insect,
If one should die, a river of tears would flow of regret.
A late bloomer who for hours would sleep and rest,
Nourished by a pacifier made of human skin and flesh.

Growing up was a time of quest and a pursuit of
identity as she grew,
'Cause she was the one in the middle and child
number two.
Her face glowed like the sun as she took her first
piano lesson,
We watched her began to find and discover her
God-given treasures,
The rainbow in her world and that indeed was
a blessing.
Baseball she detested, but puzzles, visits to the nature
center, and farm,

Were adventurous times when she explored earth's
planet and stood tall.
She was escorted and taken by young men to proms
and fancy balls.
During the years in grade school she encountered
and faced challenges,
Which caused her to exhibit and display her pride
and self worth.
Many noble deeds were accomplished throughout
the high school years,
The founder of a poetry club, a drill team, a ROTC
leader, a church pianist, etc.

An accomplished musician in the Matthews' Trio,
And a Meyerhoff scholar in attendance at UMBC.
She joined the rowing crew at school to face another
challenge and feat,
She currently is the president of CASA on the State
University campus,
Now all grown up and mature and the pride and joy
of the Matthews' family.

Just Like My Teacher

I like to play school.
I tell my friends to sit down,
Work quietly, and put away the toys
Just like my teacher.

Now it's time to say the pledge,
No, raise your right hand I say,
Just like my teacher.

Okay boys and girls,
Put away your reader,
It's math time,
Count to 100 I say,
Just like my teacher.

Put your hands down children,
You are too noisy I say,
Just like my teacher.

Children, it's time to go inside,
Line up, time out Peter Rabbit I say,
Just like my teacher.

Lunch time children,
The lights are out,
Please clear your desks I say,
Just like my teacher.

Children, it's clean-up time,
Get your things ready,

It's time to go home I say,
Just like my teacher.

Don't run children,
Red light, walk children,
Green light,
Rascal, I say,
Just like my teacher.

PENELOPE

P   Stands for "Penny," her beloved childhood name; a faithful wife weaving a garment of love, faith, praise, and good works for her Lord and King.

E   Stands for the "eyes and ears" that has yet to hear and witness what the Heavenly Father hath prepared for his daughter who loves Him.

N   Stands for a "new creature" in Christ Jesus. Her siblings and childhood friends are true witnesses to the transformation that has taken place in her life.

E   Stands for the "excellent spirit" that dwells within and works in her life.

L   Stands for " love" which is the first fruit of the spirit that Christ is perfecting in her life.

O   Stands for "orator," for God has given unto his daughter – a faithful one, the gift of speech to teach and to proclaim the gospel of good news and peace.

P   Stands for " prosperity," God spoke this promise to Joshua and to his daughter. God said that if you would meditate in His Holy Word day and night, He would make your way prosperous and that you would have good success.

E   Stands for the "enemy"- the destroyer. God says to be aware of him at all times. When your time(s) of testing comes, take shelter in Christ for He is your Ark of Safety.

The Homeless One
(In memory of the one who helped my family)

One day I was desperate for help,
So I turned to a homeless one.
I needed someone with patience to wait,
No matter how long the wait,
So I turned to a homeless one.

I needed someone who could weather the storm,
Who didn't mind making my cares his,
One who could endure no matter the test,
So I turned to a homeless one.

I needed someone who would be content to eat little,
And sleep anywhere, standing or sitting,
Someone who didn't mind being alone,
So I turned to a homeless one.

And I found in him a heart of gold and a spirit of
solitude,
In him I found a steadfastness and the patience of Job,
Someone to be trusted to fulfill a commitment.
A keeper of a promise and one whose words were true,
And that's why I looked for help in a homeless one.

The First Of A Kind

Everybody wants to be first,
First in line, the first to eat, and to speak,
First to get wealth and fame, and the first to invent.

First to fly, and the first to land in outerspace,
First to own a home and the first to buy a cell phone,
First to be born free and the first to marry a king.

But many of us become a first of a kind without
seeking it.
Adam was the first man and Eve the first woman,
Cain and Abel were the first children.

Shirley Chisholm was the first woman to run for
president,
And Thurgood Marshall became the first black
US Supreme Court Judge,
And Dr. King was the first Civil Rights Leader
Who helped to put an end to the Jim Crow Laws.

But how about the first to send His Son because
of His love,
And the first to give His life to pay for all sin,
So that all might live and have eternal life.
That indeed, is the first of a kind.

You Must Be A Teacher

You must be a teacher because...
You stand in line and raise
Your hands in public places.

You take time to explain things to
Children in the supermarket even
If their parents don't.

You buy school supplies all year long
And seldom consider it tax deductible.
Your doctor tells you to take periodic
Bathroom breaks because
Your bladder is stressed.

You take children home and pick
Them up when they've missed the bus.
You carry enough snacks to feed a host
And extra lunch money too.

You go to work when you are sick
And dispense bandaids and kleenex.
You can't pass a pencil on the ground
without picking it up.

You miss parent conferences at
Your child's school because you
Returned late from a class field trip.

You continue to work well into the night
Even when you're home and would
Work on weekends if you had a key.

You must be a teacher because ...
Even though the school board voted
Against your pay raise, you are still
Dedicated to the work you do.

Captured and Stolen From the Motherland

It was just an ordinary day,
Mothers busily went about their merry way,
Cooking and carrying baskets on their heads,
With their babies strapped on their backs.

Fathers arose early to assemble together for the big
hunt, sons went about tending their duties just beyond
the families' villages,
Young maidens happily going about carrying out
their mothers' wishes in the bustling villages.

Then suddenly the atmosphere changes,
Sons disappear with the sun overhead,
With traces of footprints left in the earth and sand,
Echoes of silence and sounds resound.

Young maidens are snatched up at mid-day,
And taken away leaving traces of garments buried in
the soil,
The laughter and songs that once flowed were
silenced,
Trouble had appeared and taken charge and chilled
the air.

Drummers sounded their alarm throughout the land,
As cries, fears, and panic penetrated the air and flooded
the villages.

Visible signs of strangers shoeprints were left imprinted
in the earth,

An unwelcomed invasion occurred throughout
the land,
Seizing sons and daughters in and around the villages.

My God, my God, what has happened?
How can this be? Where are my children?
Were questions pouring from the lips of the mothers
and fathers.
As fierce pain and sorrow gripped their hearts
and souls.

Sadness hovered over the villages like thick
dark clouds,
It was as if the sun stood still while the moon took its
place in the starry sky,
For what had started out as just an ordinary day,
Was preparing to change the course of history in
the motherland.

A Family Reunion

Oh what a great day that will be!
When all God's children of African roots,
Journey back to the motherland.
Descendants of every nation will come,
From every corner of the world, back to the homeland.

Oh for the joy that awaits the great grands!
As we discover our African heritage and the
motherland;
Releasing and letting go of unforgiveness and
bitterness,
And flooding our hearts and souls with love and
reconciliation.

Can't you see a multitude of scattered sun kissed
people,
Preparing for the exodus from estranged and
foreign lands?
Putting behind the tragic history of slavery and
suffering,
That caused massive separation of loved ones,
And reuniting families of the fourth and fifth
generations.

I see brothers and sisters coming from the tourist
attracted islands;
I see them coming from lands ruled by kings and
queens;

I see them coming from lands that have claimed domi-
nance in languages;

I see them coming from a land called America,
the Beautiful.
Oh what a great day that will be!

And the descendants keep coming,
Parading a rainbow of colors and many hues,
By way of the airways, trains, and buses,
Journeying all the way back to the motherland.
Drummers, dancers, and griots across the African
continent,
Are assembling the welcoming party,
To await their long lost love ones.
Oh what a day of rejoicing it will be!

We're gonna gather together for a great feast,
share testimonies,
And fellowship around the table in the motherland,
To celebrate the grand arrival of our kinsmen.
We're gonna tell how God brought us up and out of
bondage and slavery.
Even though we had to go through some fiery
furnaces,

Cross some red seas and toiled in tobacco, sugar cane,
and cotton fields.

But at last, we've arrived, rejoicing and giving thanks
to our God,
For a safe passage home.
We've arrived with great faith, fortitude, and patience,
And carrying the revealed glory in us,
On this great and glorious Celebration Day,
To this long, awaited family reunion.
Praise God, praise God, praise God!

Time Goes On
(A Tribute To My High School Class)

Like the greenness of a leaf,
Like a secretary without work,
And a laboratory with no apparatus,
Time continually goes on.

Like a typewriter with broken keys,
And a scientist who has no inventions,
Time never cease but goes on.

Like the cry of a new born,
And a smile of death upon an old one,
Time goes on.

From spring comes summer,
From fall comes winter,
Time old time repeatedly flows on.

What is time? Shall I say?
Be that it will or may.
Can it be achieved
Without the power to succeed?

Can it be applied knowledge,
Or that which is abolished?
Can it be a sunset which passes your block,
Or the ticking from a coo-coo clock?

Time does not reside in a clock,
Nor in the wind that blows the boat on the dock,
Be that it will or may,
Time goes on.

Time waits not for the leaders,
The blacks, the whites,
For you nor I.

The end has come for us,
Has come it must,
But time goes on.

We part, but in years to be,
Shall pleasant memories
Cling to each,
As time goes on.

Growing Up

Out of diapers,
A high chair,
A rocking horse,
A night light,
Growing up.

Baby crib removed,
Birthday party at McDonald's,
Tooth fairy's visit,
School bus stop,
Growing up.

A room remodeled,
Bicycle training wheels,
Kindergarten graduation day,
Saturday's dance class,
Growing up.

A week-end sleepover,
Shopping for school clothes,
Two weeks summer camp,
Bedtime hour extended,
Growing up.

A training bra,
Tiger Scout to Boy Scout,
Weekly chores and allowances,
Middle school classes,
Growing up.

Braces removed,
Jr.'s voice change,
Driver's ed.,
Sweet sixteen,
Growing up.

Movie night with friends,
Senior prom date,
High school graduation,
More privacy ... college
Growing up.

The Gentle Man

Guys are full of jokes and games,
They are charmers, chatters and flirts.
But I know one, full of kindness, such respect,
And I call him the gentle man.

Places I go and greet new faces,
Appearances neat, though talk is cheap.
He speaks a language from a far-off place.
His daily wear does not suit all places,
But his character stands high above the rest,
And I call him the gentle man.

A face of lines, a brow of frowns,
An honest laughter,(hey ey ey!)
Blending in a voice of dignity.
The company he keeps, a bit wonderful
To sit and listen.

I remember the day I first set out to visit,
The choice indeed mine, though it struck me funny.
The hour came and I began.
The weather was bleak and not so sunny.
I started out and then returned,
To fetch a pastel and then again the journey.

Together, we walked a step or two.
Silently I waited and entered a room.
The room, small, and masculinely arranged.
My eyes glanced toward the windows void of curtains.

To myself I uttered a word or two,
"Is this the life to let a friend live,
To prepare a strange home?' ...
Then service I'll give.
"He is my kin, and a hand in need
Is the deed to do!"

We sat and talked 'til hours passed.
I watched the rain wash the windows clean.
I thought of chores, duties and favors,
And felt a need to prepare his table.

The hour came and again I went.
Upon the windows appeared new raindrops.
My coat I received with a pleasant greeting,
Then together we walked and ended
The night's meeting.

Puddles of drops stretched on my path,
I traveled on, though my thoughts
Rested on the gentle man,
As I traveled on, though my thoughts
Rested on the gentle man.

(This poem is dedicated to Gordon, a Nigerian, whom I met in
college 2/1/1973)

A Portrait of a Teacher

A memory began at St. Joseph High
On October 28th, 1975
It was time to practice the
art of teaching.
My supervisor's expectations I
Did not know,
Or the art of authentic teaching.

Tense and worried I was
The first few days.
Among the teachers I felt uneasy,
As though I had no confidence.
Could I pretend to be something
I really wasn't?
I wondered... yes, my conscience whispered,
"Be true to thyself and make thine own mistakes."

Inspite of the uneasiness,
I had to portray a competent teacher
To the students in the coming weeks ahead.
Weeks passed, gradually my confidence built,
And so did my inner peace too.

"Prepare a plan to direct grade 12,"
my supervisor said.
Immediately I froze... seconds
Later it hit me,
The time had come to be that person
In college I set out to become.

That night and night after night
I prepared myself to meet
The needs of students in grade 12.
The day came, the prepared plan
Was put to a test.
And yet my determination over-powered
The uneasiness concealed within me.

On the first day I poured out my soul
Into the students, and set out to
Actively involve them in learning.
Weeks came and went;
Many accomplished the objectives,
With the exception of a few.
These findings were discovered
On the day I graded tests
Taken by students in grade 12.
Surprisingly, this was the picture
I framed about teaching.

The Unwanted Child

A lantern fell from the shelf,
A house burned and a babe was left;
A surviving one that cultivates indifference,
To shut out the follies of no reference.

One that seeks comfort for his weary mind,
To penetrate a dream of each and every sign.
A beg here long, and groan to know,
But all that's left is a scar to show.

A name I might someday claim,
Or decry some part of a great refrain;
To reach out for love, where I could not find,
But traces and sounds of a strange kind.

A bowed head with thoughts so dear,
Out-stretched hands for something to appear.
Live and never walk,
Maybe smile and never talk.

A body of flesh that looks like bark,
With eyes that's accustomed to gloom,
To reveal the color of a broom.

Like a bad-tempered dog who finds himself beaten.
A being, alone, to endure an unknown fate,
Never any reason to look for an open gate.

No one to share a secret,
No one to tell that milk is a liquid;
One who's in a state of shock,
No mom near to shelter and rock.

A child who sits alone.
A child who has no home;
A child who can find no one to play,
Nor hear voices saying hurray.

A figure I can't despise,
This someone who has no eyes;
Someone who has no speech of a kind,
Yet, can't find peace for his troubled mind.

Limbs that are not erect,
No tears or laughter of regret.
All the pity, the vanity, the compassion I feel,
Is for the life of this child who lives.

A child with a mental case,
But no hospital can spare space.
Help this helpless child,
One that lives near the river of Nile.

We have to justify our cause,
By reason that we will someday confess,
If we don't lament this child we need to bless.

Yes, God is our judge,
One who holds no grudge;
The case of this child is
Not on file,
But don't shut out an unwanted child.

ISAAC

I   Intelligent, influential, intuitive, and informed wise and godly son who blesses his mom and dad, and trust in an infinite God.

S   Saved, stately, and secure in his salvation

A   Athletic, artistic, and he can do ALL things through Christ who gives him the strength and the ability.

A   Alpha – the beginning and the first is his God

C   Christ is his Savior, the one who died for all of our sins; He is striving to become Christ-like to reflect His image, and his faith is in a changeless and an eternal God.

Amazing Love

Love is such an amazing thing,
It fills your heart with the joy it brings,
You soar above the highest clouds,
And dream those impossible dreams.
You hope in things unseen,
Love is such an amazing thing.

Life is full of wonder,
It showers you with excitement,
Filled with laughter, surprises, and tears.
You dance and dance through the night,
Love is such an amazing thing.

So treasure it and cherish it within your heart,
And don't ever let it depart,
Nourish it so it will continue to grow,
'Cause love is such an amazing thing,
Yes, love is such an amazing thing.

If I Knew You And You Knew Me

If I knew you and you knew me,
If both of us could clearly see,
And with an inner sight divine,
You and I would invest a few moments of time,
To understand the meaning of your heart and mine.
I'm sure that we would differ less,
'Cause we would see how compatible, thus choose the best,
And clasp our hands in friendliness,
Our minds would pleasantly agree,
And take the chance to let it be,
To allow our hearts to converse and see,
If I knew you and you knew me.

Oh How I Love Thee

The lantern in me burns for you,
Like flashes of lightening running wild.
Oh how sweetly it flows,
Like a summer stream,
Springing up through new land,
It flows and flows, giving new life ,
Creating a smile, a laughter, a dance, a song,
And a heart bursting with love.

There's Something About Him

So many thoughts go through my mind,
Rounding qualities …wasting time;
Capturing a look and a gaze in space,
Possessed by a laughter upon his face.

A touch, a welcomed embrace, revealing passion,
A kiss of truth, a blush, a moment of warmth;
Then his letting go, his good-byes…so long,
As if to say, "let's stay longer;"
He pauses…and then he's gone.

These thoughts, they linger and grow,
And for some reason my heart knows.
So it lies the end of a perfect day,
The sun's set, and the sky's dim,
As I discover that something about him.

An Expression of Love

When you're near,
Gladness is near,
When you're gone,
Sadness appear.
When you're there
And we're apart,
Something inside beats,
A beat of my heart for you.

O Come Love

O what joy in you I have,
To walk the shore, to stop to stare!
To see a face, I know you're there,
The voice I hear, it's in the air!
O Come Love.

The wind, the rain, it's starting to blow,
The whisper, the laughter, is beginning to flow!
The shadow I see, I think I know!
O Come Love.

Hello, hello big beautiful world!
Look you see I am your girl!
You are so great, so big for words,
The birds, they sing a lovely song,
O Come Love.

My arms, my arms, are here to hold,
They are to shelter you from the cold!
Let's sail upon the dancing wind,
And nestle among the starry clouds,
You are so great, so big, so bold,
O Come Love.

Did He Not Step Aside?
(College Days)

Briefly was the introduction
As we gathered near the student union,
'Viewing summer dreams and talking of classes.
Often we met 'til classes set in,
And happily we parted.
Magnetically, you and I were drawn together,
Not by love, but by his absence.
Games, dances, sunny walks,
With chance we made,
Never too soon did we once gather.

Now, he and I conceived in dreams,
And talk of classes,
Walk closer to our union.
He is here and you are far,
Scarcely do we all meet,
But happy are the two drawn together,
And never will absence cause us to part.

Syllable

Love
For him
I cannot measure
He fills my life
With moments of pleasure
And love grows
Like flowers
Blooming.

The Fleeting of Life

Out of the open page of life
Flows the freedom of choice.
Out from nature's womb
Springs a moving creature,
Staring from an open window,
I see a shadow,
Drawing near, moving closer.
My eyes watches as it moves.
I gain a sense of warmth,
A sense of belonging.
Now passing, my eyes follow,
Watching the shadow as it fades in space,
Carrying with it my dreams and the love I need.
I follow the path of the shadow,
That brought me warmth,
Rushing and running toward the
Open page of life.

I Was Walking in the Park

I was walking in the park,
When I saw a little lark,
I caught it,
I picked it up,
I put it in a cage.

I was sliding down the slide,
When I saw a cone-shape beehive,
I kicked it,
I picked it up,
I put it in a cage.

I was riding on the merry-go-round,
When I saw a baby hound,
I caught it,
I picked it up,
I put it in a cage.

I was swinging on a swing,
When I saw a shiny round ring,
I touched it,
I picked it up,
I put it in a cage.

I was climbing on the monkey bars,
When I saw a toy car,
I pushed it,
I picked it up,
I put it in a cage.

I was jumping in the sand box,
When I saw a pointed rock,
I felt it,
I picked it up,
I put it in a cage.

I was looking at my collection,
Then my brother began to cry,
Oh boy, I sighed,
I hugged him and lifted up the cage to him,
He opened up the door,
And then he took my toy.

That's Being Young
(A Day at the Park)

Watching as she turns cart wheels,
Running, skipping- free as a pony.
A group gathers all around,
Scouts I suppose
All dressed as one.

Oh look, how funny,
Dripping wet – into the pool she's fallen,
And there she stands,
Singing natural happiness,
Now that's being young!

Bubble Gum

I like to chew bubble gum.
I like to blow air in bubble gum.
I can blow big bubbles.
I can blow little bubbles.
Bubble gum smells good,
And it taste good too.
I can stretch it,
And pop it and roll it too.
Bubble gum can make sounds.
Air goes in,
Air comes out,
And pop goes the bubble,
All over my face.

Whose Shoes

Whose shoes these are,
I think I know,
His feet are jumping on the floor.
Whose shoes these are,
I think I know,
These feet are walking on the moon.
Whose shoes these are,
I think I know,
Her feet are dancing in mid-air.
Whose shoes these are,
I think I know,
These feet are skating on the ice.
Whose shoes these are,
I think I know,
A horse of course!

Spring

Spring into season, thus begin a new day,
It's a time for new life, happiness and play.
The sun is bright, the grass is green,
The trees are tall, indeed a splendid scene,
All is as beautiful as it seems.

Fun
(A Child At Heart)

Fun is hitting a home run and
Winning the baseball game.
Fun is making mud pies and
Building sand castles in the sand.
Fun is rolling down a country hill and
Fishing with a homemade rod at the lake.

Fun is playing hop scotch and
Jump rope on a hot summer day.
Fun is swinging on a swing at the local park.
Fun is playing hide-go-seek with
Your sisters and brothers and no one finds you.

Fun is telling jokes and laughing
So hard until you cry tears of joy.
Fun is playing in an April shower and
Getting soaked from head to toe,
And gathering and smelling honey suckles.
Fun is taking your bedding outside
To camp in your front yard to look up
To watch and count the stars at night.

Fun is discovering new things, creating new songs,
Blowing bubbles, whistling, and chewing bubble gum,
Drawing and learning how to read.
Fun is when you first realize that you like boys
If you're a girl, and having a crush on a girl
If you're a boy.
Fun is sweet dreams that you wish would last forever.

I Love You Just That Much Mom

I love you as much as the sky is high,
I love you as much as the ocean is deep,
I love you as much as the wind that blows,
Mom I love you just that much!

I love you as much as the stars that twinkles,
I love you as much as the sun that shines,
I love you as much as the rain that falls from the sky,
Mom I love you just that much!

I love you as much as night turns to day,
I love you as much as winter turns to summer,
And spring turns to autumn,
Mom I love you just that much!

I love you as much as the clouds in the sky,
I love you as much as the honey in the cone,
I love you as much as my heart that beats,
Mom I love you just that much!

A Sorority Pledge

I am an Ivy of AKA,
I pledged to you on a Saturday,
I made a vow 'tis true' to keep.
I'll serve you loyal dear AKA,
I'll serve you long dear AKA.
With tribute to you I'll give,
And honor to you I'll live.
I "Ivy Brandy" wish to say,
I am a sister of AKA.

College Days

In the morn when I wake,
I wash my face to overtake;
When mid-noon rolls around,
I seek for food and settle down;
Nearing evening I make my routes,
Classes over and times out;
But comes night when sleep falls,
I rest my body and my soul,
And say night night to God and all.

We Love To Write

We love to write,
We love to write,
We love to write,
And read to you;
And when we write,
We learn so much more,
And have fun along the way.

Eeny meeny miny moe,
Let's just all decide
To grow,
To read, to write
With all our might.
Use your mind,
And take your time.
Eeny meeny miny moe,
I dare you to make
It so!

(Dedicated to young writers)

A Leaf Poem

Fly high little leaf,
Touch the sky.
Let Mr. Wind take you far,
Over the hills,
To the moon,
Far away to new lands.
You're free!
And in spring
Come back and visit me.

A Pumpkin Shape

Pumpkins are round,
Pumpkins are orange,
Pumpkins are found on the ground.

A Jack-O-Lantern

Big ones, little ones, round ones too.
Pumpkins, pumpkins, just for you.
Pick one, carve one, what a treat!
Pumpkins, pumpkins, you're so neat!

A Pumpkin Rhyme

I like pumpkins
I like mice,
I like a story that's nice!

A Pumpkin Pie

Pumpkin, pumpkin, grow and grow.
Change your colors, oh so slow!
Pumpkin, pumpkin, what can you be?
I'll hide you on Halloween,
And eat you for my treat!

The Pumpkin Patch

Pumpkin, pumpkin orange and fat,
I'll pick you from the pumpkin patch.
Pumpkin, pumpkin full of seeds,
Full of color and oh so sweet!
Come home with me to be my treat!

A Pumpkin Rap
A Youth Opera

This thing's a pumpkin
Did you know?
It changes colors,
I watched it grow.
It's vines are long,
It's vines are leafy.
Inside the pumpkin
Is stuff to eat.
Let's clean the thing,
Let's bake the seeds.
Say bye-bye to the pumpkin patch,
Say bye-bye to Halloween,
'Cause I'm gonna make
You my treat, treat, treat!

Ezra Pound Couplet

Wondering
A mouse roaming in a corn field,
A child lost in a shopping center.

Form

Drifting, lingering, calmly, coasting
Slumbering, weeping, groaning
Patiently, changing, shifting
Rising, moving, sailing, onward.

Thomas Couplet

Did you ever see a flower?
Brightly blooming, fully formed, gently
Unfolding.

Did you ever see a bus?
Rapidly rolling, closely steered, completely
Filled.

Haiku

He searched his soul deeply,
Thinking every second, minute, day, and week,
Attending church and asking blessings.

Love

A need to fulfill loneliness,
To hold not delusion to face everlasting,
Yet lingers after a loved one passes.
A delightful feeling of impermanence,
Once it's gone you find yourself somewhat solemn.

A possible loyalty that cannot be bought,
A desire every youth feels once it's caught.
A feeling born of infinite concern,
That's nourished in providential care,
An emotion that everyone experiences and shares.

Love is kind, yet hate is easier to define;
Love is a sacred joy,
Secured by every girl and boy.
Filled with some lightness from a miracle afar,
A brightness that evolves when you see a star.

A heart that standeth in awe of words,
So pleasant as a singing mocking bird.
A kiss that ponders on the mouth,
So sensational without a doubt!
Days of happiness with heart-felt dreams,
And eyes that answer with flickering beams.

A loving touch of a cheek,
Flushed by the inviting lips to meet.
Love can be found, when lost it comes again,
Like a stream, love expands.

An unhindered passion that will endure,
And one whose emotion is pure.
Love returns on the rebound,
A spirit crying to be found,
A flowing compassion in all mankind.

Like a blazing fire no one can deny,
Yet blind as a hidden eye,
It expands the dimensions of the soul,
With every imagination untold,
And seeketh to capture a heart of gold.

Something not yours or mine,
Love is independent and divine.
Love is natural and ordinary,
When untrue, love's contrary.
Envy, agony, and pain,
They all torture you in vain.
An outpour of doves from above,
Life is nothing without love.

Printed in the United States
64454LVS00001B/157-1500